The Battle Over Homework

The Practicing Administrator's Leadership Series
Jerry J. Herman and Janice L. Herman, Editors

ROADMAPS
TO SUCCESS

Other Titles in This Series Include:

The Battle Over Homework

An Administrator's Guide to Setting Sound and Effective Policies

Harris Cooper

CORWIN PRESS, INC.
A Sage Publications Company
Thousand Oaks, California

For information address:

Corwin Press, Inc.
A Sage Publications Company
2455 Teller Road
Thousand Oaks, California 91320

SAGE Publications Ltd.
6 Bonhill Street
London EC2A 4PU
United Kingdom

SAGE Publications India Pvt. Ltd.
M-32 Market
Greater Kailash I
New Delhi 110 048 India

Printed in the United States of America

Library of Congress Cataloging-in-Publication Data

Cooper, Harris
    The battle over homework: an administrator's guide to setting sound and effective policies / Harris Cooper.
        p.   cm. — (Roadmaps to success)
    Includes bibliographical references.
    ISBN 0–8039–6163–4 (pbk.)
    1. Homework.   I. Title.   II. Series.
LB1048.C655   1994
371.3'028'12—dc20   94–17155

94 95 96 97 98 10 9 8 7 6 5 4 3 2 1

Corwin Press Production Editor: S. Marlene Head

Contents

Foreword

For many years, homework has been a topic of heated public discussion as well as a continuing concern of students, parents, teachers, and administrators alike. How much and what kinds of homework should be given? Should parents be expected to supervise it? When a student has many teachers, should each teacher coordinate his or her homework assignments with the student's other teachers? Should administrators publish and distribute homework guidelines? Should boards of education have policies on homework? Perhaps the most crucial question of all may be, "Does homework work?"

In *The Battle Over Homework: An Administrator's Guide to Setting Sound and Effective Policies*, Harris Cooper combines the results of research studies and exemplary practices to provide guidance for those who seek intelligent, thoughtful solutions to these and other questions about homework. He discusses the effects of homework, explores variations in the homework process, and shows how to develop and implement policy guidelines. For readers who wish to delve more deeply into the subject, an annotated bibliography and references are provided following the text.

Teachers, principals, superintendents, and school board members will find this clearly written, practical volume an essential guidebook for making homework assignments both useful and meaningful.

JERRY J. HERMAN
JANICE L. HERMAN
Series Co-Editors

Preface

How much time should children spend doing homework? Should elementary schoolchildren do any homework at all? Do high or low achievers benefit most from homework? What role should parents play in the homework process?

Homework is a source of friction between home and school more often than any other teaching activity. Parents protest that assignments are too long or too short, too hard or too easy, or too ambiguous. Teachers complain about a lack of support from parents and administrators, a lack of training, and a lack of time to prepare effective assignments. Students gripe about the time homework takes from their leisure activities, if they understand the value of the exercise at all.

These complaints are not surprising, considering that homework assignments are influenced by more factors than any other instructional strategy. Teachers can structure and monitor homework in many ways. Student differences play a major role because homework allows students considerable discretion about whether, when, and how to complete assignments. The home environment influences the process by creating an atmosphere conducive to, or inhibitive of, study. Finally, the broader community plays a role by providing other leisure activities that compete for the student's time.

This book is meant to help administrators better understand the issues involved in homework. It will give administrators a sound basis for discussing homework with their faculty, students, and parents and for creating homework guidelines and policies that are fair, consistent, and based on the best available evidence.

The book addresses homework issues at both the elementary and secondary levels. Differences in the value of homework at different grade levels, as we shall see, are among homework's most interesting and revealing aspects.

The role of research in forming the homework attitudes and practices of teachers, parents, and policymakers has been minimal. This is because the influences on homework are complex—no simple, general finding proving or disproving its utility is possible. However, research is plentiful enough that a few studies can be found to promote whatever position is desired, while the counterevidence is ignored. Thus advocates for or against homework often cite isolated studies either to support or to refute its value.

Because I firmly believe that research can positively influence educational policy and practice, I have tried to avoid these shortcomings in developing the conclusions and recommendations contained in this book. In preparation for writing this book, I attempted to collect all research, both positive and negative, conducted in the past 50 years that examined the effects of homework or that compared variations in homework assignments, processes, and contexts. I then applied the most rigorous techniques to integrate the results of studies, using statistical procedures where possible (see Cooper & Hedges, 1994).

The book is divided into five chapters. The first chapter contains (a) a general definition of homework; (b) the important distinctions in homework assignments; (c) a list of the possible effects of homework, both positive and negative; and (d) a model of the homework process. Chapter 2 summarizes research on whether homework is generally effective, as well as whether it is more effective for some grade levels, subjects, and types of students than for others. Chapter 3 looks at research on how much homework is optimal for students at different grades. Studies of variations in homework assignments that can influence their effects on achievement are examined in chapter 4. Particular attention is paid to the structure of assignments, the need to be responsive to student individual differences, the role of home and community factors, and the value of classroom follow-up, such as grading and feedback. The final chapter reviews some of the policy recommendations offered by government and private education agencies. These recommendations and the discussions of previous chapters are then integrated into a set of homework policy guidelines for school districts, buildings, and classrooms.

My involvement with homework began in 1986. In that year I received a grant from the National Science Foundation to gather, summarize, and integrate the research on the effects of homework. Before I began, I had no strong predisposition favoring or opposing homework. I did have much experience with rigorous techniques for summarizing research literatures. Ultimately, my research synthesis would include nearly 120 studies, would require me to read about two times that many related nonempirical pieces on homework, and would result in the first book-length assessment of homework as a pedagogical device (titled, not surprisingly, *Homework*). Since that book was published, I have spent hundreds of hours talking with principals, teachers, parents, and students about homework. Those discussions, along with the writings of researchers and practicing educators, inform the contents of the pages that follow.

HARRIS COOPER

About the Author

Harris Cooper is the Frederick A. Middlebush Professor of Psychology and a research associate of the Center for Research in Social Behavior at the University of Missouri—Columbia. He received his Ph.D. in social psychology from the University of Connecticut and has been a visiting scholar at Harvard University, Stanford University, the University of Oregon, and the Russell Sage Foundation. He is also an elected member of the Columbia, MO, Board of Education.

Harris Cooper studies the application of social psychology to educational policy issues. In 1989, he published *Homework*, the first book-length analysis of research on homework's effects. He has also published one book and over two dozen articles and book chapters on teacher expectation effects. In addition, he has written on the policy implications of research concerning class size, desegregation, and corporal punishment.

He is also interested in methods of research synthesis. He is author of two books on procedures for conducting scientific reviews of research literature.

Harris Cooper has been an advising editor for the *Journal of Educational Psychology*, the *Elementary School Journal*, the *Journal of Experimental Education*, and the *Personality and Social Psychology Bulletin*. He was the first recipient of the American Educational Research Association's Early Career Award for Programmatic Research.

Homework: Finding the Common Ground

Attitudes Toward Homework

At any moment during the past century, the educational literature has contained contemporaneous arguments for and against homework. However, at different times the proponents and opponents of homework have alternately held sway.

Early in the 20th century, homework was believed to be an important means for disciplining children's minds. The mind was viewed as a muscle. Memorization—most often of material like multiplication tables, names, and dates—not only led to knowledge acquisition but was also a good mental exercise. Because memorization could be accomplished easily at home, homework was a key schooling strategy.

By the 1940s, a reaction against homework set in. Developing problem-solving ability, as opposed to learning through drill, became a central task of education. The use of homework as punishment or to enhance memorization skills was called into question. Greater emphasis was placed on developing student initiative and interest in learning. Also, the life-adjustment movement viewed home study as an intrusion on students' time to pursue other private, at-home activities.

The trend toward less homework was reversed in the late 1950s after the Russians launched the Sputnik satellite. Americans became concerned that a lack of rigor in the educational system was leaving children unprepared to face a complex technological future and to compete against our ideological adversaries. Homework was viewed as a means for accelerating the pace of knowledge acquisition.

By the mid-1960s the cycle again reversed itself. Homework came to be seem as a symptom of too much pressure on students to achieve. Contemporary learning theories were cited that questioned the value of most approaches to homework. And yet again, the possible detrimental mental health consequences of too much homework were brought to the fore. For example, Wildman wrote in a 1968 article, "Whenever homework crowds out social experience, outdoor recreation, and creative activities, and whenever it usurps time devoted to sleep, it is not meeting the basic needs of children and adolescents" (p. 203).

Today, views of homework have shifted once more toward a more positive assessment. In the wake of declining achievement test scores and increasing concern for traditional family values, public perception of the value of homework has undergone its third renaissance in the past 50 years.

A Definition of Homework

Homework is defined as tasks assigned to students by schoolteachers that are intended to be carried out during nonschool hours. The word *intended* is used because students may complete homework assignments during study hall, library time, or even during subsequent classes. However, this definition explicitly excludes (a) in-school guided study; (b) home study courses delivered through the mail, television, or on audio- or videocassette; and (c) extracurricular activities such as sports teams and clubs.

Homework can be classified according to its (a) amount, (b) purpose, (c) skill area, (d) degree of individualization, (e) degree of

TABLE 1.1 Distinctions in Homework Assignments

Classification	Within Classification
Amount	Frequency
	Length
Purpose	Instructional
	Practice
	Preparation
	Extension
	Integration
	Noninstructional
	Parent-child communication
	Fulfilling directives
	Punishment
	Community relations
Skill area used	Writing
	Reading
	Memory or retention
Degree of individualization	Geared to individual student
	Geared to groups of students
Degree of student choice	Compulsory
	With task options
	Voluntary
Completion deadlines	Long-term
	Short-term
Social context	Independent
	Assisted (parent, sibling, other)
	Student group

choice for the student, (f) completion deadline, and (g) social context. Table 1.1 summarizes the distinctions in homework.

The *amount* of homework simply refers to the frequency with which homework is assigned and/or the length of particular assignments.

The *purposes* of a homework assignment can be divided into instructional and noninstructional objectives (cf. Lee & Pruitt, 1979).

Four instructional goals are most often identified for homework. The first and most common purpose of homework is practice or review. Practice assignments are meant to reinforce the learning of material already presented in class and to help students master specific skills.

Secondly, preparation assignments introduce material to be presented in subsequent lessons. Their aim is to help students obtain the maximum benefit when the new material is covered in class by providing background information or experiences. Quite often the difference between practice and preparation homework is not in the content of the assignment but in its temporal relation to the material being covered in class—the same material presented before class discussion is preparation, whereas after class discussion it is practice or review. Some homework assignments can have both practice and preparation objectives by introducing new material along with old.

The third instructional goal for homework is called extension. Extension homework involves the transfer of previously learned skills to new situations. This often requires the application of abstract principles in circumstances not covered in class. For example, students might learn about the factors that led to the French Revolution and be asked to apply them to other revolutions.

Finally, homework can serve the purpose of integration. Integrative homework requires the student to apply many separately learned skills and concepts to produce a single product. Examples might include book reports, science projects, or creative writing.

There are other purposes of homework in addition to enhancing instruction. For example, homework can be used to (a) establish communication between parent and child, (b) fulfill directives from school administrators, and (c) punish students. To this list might be added the public relations objective of simply informing parents about what is going on in school.

Homework assignments rarely reflect a single purpose. Instead, most assignments have elements of several different purposes. Some of these relate to instruction, whereas others may meet the purposes of the teacher, the school administration, or even the school district.

In addition to differences in purpose, homework can call for the use of different skills. Students may be asked to read, submit written products, or perform drill to enhance memory or retention of material. Written products are often required to provide evidence that the assignment was completed. Drill activities involve mechanical, repetitive exercises. These might include, for example, practicing multiplication tables or rehearsing a public speech.

The degree of individualization refers to whether the teacher tailors assignments to meet the needs of each student or whether a single assignment is presented to groups of students or the class as a whole.

The degree of choice afforded a student refers to whether the homework assignment is compulsory or voluntary. Within compulsory homework assignments, students can be given different degrees of discretion concerning which or how many parts of the assignment to complete.

Related to the degree of choice is the fact that completion deadlines for homework assignments can also vary. Some assignments are short-term and are meant to be completed overnight or for the next class meeting. Other assignments are long-term, with students given perhaps a week or several weeks to complete the task.

Finally, homework assignments can vary according to the social context in which they are carried out. Some assignments are meant to be completed by the student independently of other people. Assisted homework explicitly calls for the involvement of another person, typically a parent but perhaps a sibling or a friend. Still other assignments involve groups of students working cooperatively to produce a single product.

The Effects of Homework

As might be expected, educators have suggested a long list of both positive and negative consequences of homework. These are listed in Table 1.2.

Positive Effects

The positive effects of homework can be grouped into four categories: (a) immediate academic effects, (b) long-term academic effects, (c) nonacademic effects, and (d) parental involvement effects. The immediate effects of homework on learning are the most

TABLE 1.2 Positive and Negative Effects of Homework

Effects of Homework

Positive

Immediate achievement and learning
  Better retention of factual knowledge
  Increased understanding
  Better critical thinking, concept formation, information processing
  Curriculum enrichment

Long-term academic
  Encourage learning during leisure time
  Improved attitude toward school
  Better study habits and skills

Nonacademic
  Greater self-direction
  Greater self-discipline
  Better time organization
  More inquisitiveness
  More independent problem solving

Greater parental appreciation of, and involvement in, schooling

Negative

Satiation
  Loss of interest in academic material
  Physical and emotional fatigue

Denial of access to leisure time and community activities

Parental interference
  Pressure to complete and perform well
  Confusion of instructional techniques

Cheating
  Copying from other students
  Help beyond tutoring

Increased differences between high and low achievers

frequent rationales for assigning homework. Proponents of homework argue that it increases the time students spend on academic tasks. As such, the benefits of increased instructional time should accrue to students engaged in home study. Regardless of the theoretical rationale, among the suggested positive academic effects of homework are (a) better retention of factual knowledge; (b) increased understanding of material; (c) better critical-thinking, concept-formation, and information- processing skills; and (d) enrichment of the core curriculum. Obviously, all these benefits will not accompany any single homework assignment. Instead, assignments can be tailored to promote one or more of these outcomes.

The long-term academic consequences of homework are not necessarily enhancements to achievement in particular academic domains but rather the establishment of general student practices that facilitate learning. Homework is therefore expected to (a) encourage students to learn during their leisure time, (b) improve students' attitudes toward school, and (c) improve students' study habits and skills. Homework has also been offered as a means for developing personal attributes in children that extend beyond academic pursuits. Because homework generally requires students to complete tasks with less supervision and under less severe time constraints than is the case in school, home study is said to promote greater self-discipline and self-direction, better time organization, more inquisitiveness, and more independent problem solving. These skills and attributes apply both to the nonacademic and the academic spheres of life.

Homework may also have positive effects for the parents of schoolchildren. By having students bring work home for parents to see and perhaps by requesting that parents take part in the process, teachers can use homework to increase parents' appreciation of, and involvement in, schooling. Parental involvement may have positive effects on children as well. Students become aware of the connection between home and school. Parents can demonstrate an interest in the academic progress of their children.

Negative Effects

Some of the negative effects attributed to home study contradict the suggested positive effects. For instance, although some have argued that homework can improve students' attitudes toward school, others counter that attitudes may be influenced negatively. They appeal to what is called a "satiation effect" as the underlying cause; that is, they argue that the potential is limited for any activity to remain rewarding. By spending increased time on school learning, children may become overexposed to academic tasks. Thus homework may undermine good attitudes and strong achievement motivation.

Related to the satiation argument are the notions that homework leads to general physical and emotional fatigue and denies access to leisure time and community activities. Proponents of leisure activities point out that doing homework is not the only circumstance under which after-school learning takes place. Many leisure-time activities teach important academic and life skills. The key is to find the proper balance of leisure and learning.

Involving parents in the schooling process can have negative consequences. Sometimes parents pressure students to complete homework assignments or to do them with unrealistic rigor. Also, parents may create confusion if they are unfamiliar with the material that is sent home for study or if their approach to learning differs from that taught in school.

In addition, parental involvement in homework can sometimes go beyond simple tutoring or assistance. This raises the possibility that homework might promote cheating or an overreliance on others for help with assignments. Although a lack of supervision can enhance self-direction and self-discipline, it may also lead some students to copy assignments or to receive inappropriate help from others.

Some opponents of homework have argued that home study has increased differences between high- and low-achieving students, especially when the achievement difference is associated with economic differences. They suggest that high achievers from well-to-do homes will have greater parental support for home study, including more appropriate parental assistance. Also, these students more likely will have quiet, well-lit places in which to do assignments and better resources to help them complete assignments successfully.

With a few exceptions, the positive and negative consequences of homework can occur together. For instance, homework can improve study habits at the same time that it denies access to other leisure-time activities. Some types of assignments can produce positive effects, whereas other assignments produce negative ones. In fact, in light of the host of ways homework assignments can be construed and carried out, complex patterns of effects ought to be expected.

Factors Affecting the Utility of Homework

Table 1.3 presents a model of the homework process. The model is an attempt to organize into a single scheme all of the factors that educators have suggested might influence the success of a homework assignment.

Not surprisingly, the model divides the homework process into two classroom phases with a home-community phase sandwiched between. Student ability and other individual differences (e.g., age, gender, economic background) and subject matter are viewed as exogenous factors or "given" conditions that can influence the homework process. In addition, the model includes the characteristics of the assignment (described above) as potential influences on homework's effectiveness. Table 1.3 also includes the potential consequences of homework as the final outcomes in the process.

The model can focus discussions of homework among administrators, teachers, parents, and students. It can be especially useful in identifying the factors that most influence the success of homework within a particular district, school, or classroom.

TABLE 1.3 A Model of Factors Influencing the Effect of Homework

Exogeneous Factors	Assignment Characteristics	Initial Classroom Factors	Home-Community Factors	Classroom Follow-Up	Outcomes or Effects
Student characteristics	Amount	Provision of materials	Competitors for student time	Feedback Written comments	Assignment completion
Ability	Purpose	Facilitators	Home environment	Grading Incentives	Assignment performance
Motivation	Skill area used	Suggested approaches	Space Light		Positive effects
Study habits		Links to curriculum	Quiet Materials	Testing of related content	Immediate academic
Subject matter	Degree of individualization	Other rationales			Long-term academic
Grade level			Others' involvement	Use in class discussion	Nonacademic
	Degree of student choice		Parents Siblings Other students		Parental
					Negative effects
	Completion deadlines				Satiation
					Denial of leisure time
					Parental interference
	Social context				Cheating
					Increased student differences

Does Homework Work?

The initial response to the question "Does homework work?" must be "Compared to what?" One way to assess homework's effectiveness would be to compare the achievement and attitudes of students who are assigned homework with students who received no homework or any other treatment meant to compensate for their lack of home study. Such comparisons would treat all students identically during school hours and have some students, but not all, complete additional academic work during nonschool hours. An alternative approach would be to compare homework with in-school supervised study. Here some students would do homework assignments at home (after school), and others would do the same assignments during class, during study hall, or during additional instructional time at school. Both types of comparisons have been used to assess the effectiveness of homework.

Homework Versus No Homework

I was able to find 17 research reports appearing since 1962 that detailed the results of studies involving comparisons of homework and no-homework classrooms. The studies included over 3,300 students in 85 classrooms and 30 schools in 11 states. The studies contained a total of 48 usable comparisons.

Of the 48 comparisons, 18 used class tests or grades as the outcome measure for homework and 30 used standardized achievement tests. Twenty-five comparisons involved achievement in mathematics, 13 looked at reading and English, and 10 involved science and social studies. The duration of the homework treatments varied considerably from study to study. The length of studies ranged from 2 to 30 weeks, averaging between 9 and 10 weeks.

Is Homework Better Than No Homework at All?

Yes. About 70% of comparisons indicated a positive effect for homework. More precisely, the average student in these studies doing homework had a higher achievement score than 55% of students not doing homework. However, there were several important qualifiers to this general conclusion.

Do Homework Effects Vary With Grade Level?

Yes. The positive effect of homework varied markedly for students at different grades—older students benefited most from doing homework. The average effect of homework was twice as large for high school than for junior high school students, and twice as large again for junior high than for elementary school students. Again, to make this finding more precise, teachers of Grades 4 to 6 might expect the average student doing homework to outscore about 52% of equivalent no-homework students. For junior high students the equivalent expectation would be about 60%, and about 69% for high school students.

What About Other Student Differences?

Comparisons of homework effects on students who differed on variables other than grade level or age generally showed no difference. Specifically, I found seven studies in which researchers looked at whether the effects of homework were different for males and females and four studies that examined intelligence. These revealed no consistent pattern of results.

Is Subject Matter Important?

Subject matter influenced the outcome of comparisons a bit, and in a somewhat counterintuitive manner. Comparisons involving mathematics revealed the smallest effect of homework, those involving science and social studies revealed the largest effect, and those involving reading and English fell in the middle. When comparisons involving the different subskills of mathematics were made, homework appeared to affect problem solving less than computational or conceptual skills. However, because these findings were not consistent with some other findings described subsequently, I prefer to interpret them with caution.

Does Homework Affect All Achievement Measures Equally?

No. How achievement was measured was significantly related to the outcome of homework versus no-homework comparisons. Homework had a larger effect when achievement was measured by class tests or grades than when it was measured by standardized tests. This seems logical, considering that material on homework assignments should correspond more closely to material that was taught in class and that appeared on tests than to content covered on more general achievement tests. However, the next chapter shows that there was no difference between standardized and teacher-developed achievement measures when the effects of time spent on homework are at issue. These studies indicate standardized measures and teacher-constructed measures can differ in trustworthiness: Standardized measures may be generally more trustworthy than teacher-constructed ones. Thus we might expect the effect of homework to be relatively equal on self-developed and standardized measures of achievement, although the mechanisms producing these results might be quite different.

What About the Frequency and Length of Assignments?

It is no surprise that homework produced larger positive effects if students did more assignments per week. Surprisingly, the effect of homework was negatively related to the duration of the homework treatment: Treatments spanning longer periods produced less of a homework effect. These longer treatments may have involved less frequent homework assignments during any given week, thereby dissipating its effect.

Does Homework Affect Students' Attitudes?

I found only three studies that involved comparisons of the attitudes of students doing and not doing homework. These studies were conducted on third through sixth and ninth graders. The results of all three studies suggest that homework has neither a positive nor a negative effect on students' attitudes toward school, teacher, or subject matter.

Homework Versus In-School Supervised Study

In the studies reviewed so far, no-homework students received no instruction meant to compensate for their lack of home study. In the studies that follow, the no-homework students were required to engage in some form of in-school supervised study not required of students doing homework. Thus these studies compare the effects of two different treatments.

The definition of in-school supervised study varied from experiment to experiment. Essentially, three characteristics of the treatment are most germane. First, some researchers have examined the effects of homework compared to added study time at school. This has been accomplished by lengthening the school day or by shortening the time devoted to subjects or activities not covered in the homework assignments. Second, the type of supervision given students in the no-homework group has ranged from passive to active. Finally, supervised study can differ in regard to how closely its content corresponds to that required of the students doing homework. In some studies the content was identical, whereas in other studies the material in the two treatments was related but not identical.

My search of the literature located eight studies conducted in the past 25 years comparing homework and in-school supervised study. These studies contained 18 comparisons of the two treatments, based on 10 independent samples containing a total of over 1,000 students in 40 classrooms and 10 schools in six states. Because this set of comparisons is based on a considerably smaller number of studies than those involving homework and no-homework groups, I was not able to test as many hypotheses about moderating influences as I was in the prior comparison. Also, these results must be viewed with more caution.

Is Homework Better Than In-School Study?

Yes. That is what the studies generally indicated. Across the 10 independent samples, the average student in the homework condition outperformed about 53.6% of the supervised-study students. This is a smaller effect than was found in comparisons of homework versus no-homework studies. Given that these studies are really comparing two alternate treatments, this is not a surprising result. It is easy to imagine ways to manipulate homework assignments and/or the definition of supervised study to produce results favoring one treatment or the other.

However, I must qualify the overall conclusion.

Does Grade Level Influence Effects of the Two Strategies?

Yes. When I compared results according to elementary school (Grades 5 and 6), junior high (Grades 7 to 9), and high school, I found an important relationship. Supervised study had a more positive effect than homework on the achievement of elementary students, whereas homework was more effective for junior high and high school students.

What About Subject Matter?

The subject matter considered in a study had no relation to the relative effect of homework versus in-school study. Curiously, the ordering of effects for different subjects was opposite to that for the homework versus no-homework comparisons. Considering this finding and other evidence to be described below, I would suggest that we should expect larger positive effects of homework on the learning of simple skills that require practice and rehearsal than on complex tasks that require higher order integration of knowledge and skills. It should be kept in mind, however, that this effect may again be a matter of measurement trustworthiness, because simple skills can generally be measured with less error than complex ones. It also does not rule out the use of homework that requires the integration of skills (e.g., research reports) or imagination (e.g., creative writing). The finding suggests that such assignments should build on skills that are already well learned.

Is the Type of Achievement Measure Important?

There was no relation between the type of achievement measure used in a study and the comparison's outcome. However, the size of this literature was small, so the tests of difference were weak, and many interesting potential influences could not even be examined.

What About Nonacademic Outcomes?

In two investigations, researchers looked at student attitudes as a function of homework versus in-class supervised study. One study (Hudson, 1965) showed that attitudes toward school were more favorable in the homework treatment group, whereas the other study (Tupesis, 1972) indicated identical attitudes toward the subject matter expressed by both groups. Although the different results might be explainable by the various attitude referents, there are also numerous other methodological and contextual differences between the studies.

Finally, one researcher (Hudson, 1965) found better study mechanics and time allocation among students doing homework than among students doing in-class study. This is the only study I found of the use of study habits as a measured outcome of homework.

Homework for Students With Learning Disabilities

In recent years, considerable attention has been paid to the role of homework in the education of students with learning disabilities. When I reviewed the research on homework that had appeared before 1986, I found few studies that included students with learning disabilities, either as the population of interest or for purposes of comparison. The situation today has improved somewhat, and a colleague and I recently conducted such a review (Cooper & Nye, in press). We were interested in how homework practices and policies that proved effective for students without disabilities might differ for students with disabilities.

First, we reviewed studies assessing the overall effectiveness of homework for students with learning disabilities. These studies indicated no reason to believe that the generally positive effects of homework for students without disabilities would not also appear for students with learning disabilities.

Clearly, however, the parameters of successful homework assignments are different for the two types of students. For example, a consistent theme in the literature is that homework assignments for students with learning disabilities should be short and should focus on reinforcement of skills and class lessons, as opposed to integration and extension. Also, students who fall below a minimum competency in a skill area may not benefit from homework at all.

Monitoring of homework assignments by teachers is critical for students with learning disabilities. Monitoring might consist of prompt in-class review, prominent rewards for completion and/or accuracy, and the use of class time to begin assignments, so that teachers can ensure that students understand the assignment.

Parent involvement is crucial for students with disabilities, primarily because these students are likely to have less developed self-management and study skills. Their ability to study depends more on the provision of a proper environment, both physical and emotional. Students with learning disabilities may need periodic rewards during homework time or immediately following assignment completion as well as more assistance to complete tasks. Evidence suggests that this involvement should be sustained, not discrete or periodic.

Interpreting the Magnitude of Homework's Effect

In the previous section, I discussed the relative effect of homework across different grade levels, types of outcomes, and content areas. The consequences of homework can also be compared to those of other instructional techniques. This allows the placing of homework into a broader educational context, thus permitting a more informed judgment of its value.

The third edition of the *Handbook of Research on Teaching* contained an article by Walberg (1986), who presented the results of 11 reviews of research examining the effect of instructional strategies and teaching skills on measures of student achievement. The instructional strategies included individualized, special, and cooperative learning; ability grouping; direct and programmed instruction; advance organizers; higher level cognitive questioning; use of praise; use of pretests; and television watching. Each strategy had associated with it an effect similar to the one I used previously (e.g., the average student doing homework outperformed 55% of students not doing homework). Based on a comparison with these instructional strategies, the effect of homework on achievement can best be described as above average. That is, homework's effect fell about in the middle of the 11 strategies. If grade level is taken into account, homework's effect on achievement of elementary school students could be described as small, but on high school students its effect would be large, relative to the effect of other instructional techniques.

Another aid in interpreting the magnitude of an effect is to compare it to the cost of implementing the treatment. Homework certainly can be regarded as a low-cost treatment. The major costs involved in giving homework assignments would be (a) a small loss in instructional class time because time must be allocated to homework management and (b) additional outside-class preparation and management time for teachers.

Summary

In sum, the effect of homework on the achievement of young children appears to be small, even bordering on trivial. However, for high school students the effect of homework can be impressive. Indeed, relative to other instructional techniques and the costs involved in implementation, homework can produce a substantial positive effect on adolescents' performance in school. In addition, the benefits of homework for students with learning disabilities can be great, but its success lies in (a) teacher preparation and planning; (b) assignments that are appropriate to the skill, attention, and motivation levels of students; and (c) appropriate use of parents.

Time Spent on
Homework Assignments

In the past 30 years, over half a million students have been asked to report the time they spend on homework, and their response has been related to some measure of academic achievement. Although such surveys can contain a wealth of information, they also have problems. The major problem is that the results can show that homework and achievement are related but cannot show which, if either, causes the other. So, if time spent on homework and achievement increase together, does this mean that homework improves school performance or that teachers assign more homework to better students? If more homework time is associated with lower achievement, does homework have a detrimental effect on performance, or do brighter students simply finish assignments in less time? Both positive and negative correlations have been found in past research (although positive correlations dominate), and, not surprisingly, each of the four interpretations has been invoked to make sense of the data. It is also possible that a third variable, say the economic conditions of the communities in which schools are located, causes both the students' achievement and the amount of homework.

Another problem is that the research on time and homework does not distinguish between the amount of homework teachers assign and the amount of time students spend on homework. I could find no study that attempted to separate these variables. Finally, studies of time spent on homework typically rely on the self-reports of students. The accuracy of these may be questionable, possibly influenced by an upward bias.

This chapter is divided into two main sections. First, the results of studies in which researchers calculated the simple correlation between time spent on homework and student achievement or attitude are examined. As part of this analysis, I look at several influences on the simple relation, including grade level, subject matter, and type of achievement measure. I also look separately at studies of whether more time on homework actually causes higher achievement. Second, studies will be examined that allowed me to explore whether there is an optimum amount of homework for students at different grade levels; that is, whether homework is good up to a point but then has diminishing effectiveness.

The Simple Relation Between Homework Time and Academic Outcomes

I located 17 studies of the relation between homework time and a measure of achievement or attitude. The studies contained a total of 50 correlations, because data were often analyzed separately for different subsamples of students, subjects, grades, and/or outcome measures. At least six nationwide surveys involving random samples of students have contained questions about time spent on homework, including several phases of the National Assessment of Educational Progress, the National Assessment in Science, and High School and Beyond. The nationwide surveys have been complemented by statewide surveys conducted in California, North Carolina, Pennsylvania, Rhode Island, and Washington, and by numerous school districts. A total of 112,714 students were included in the surveys.

.39,	.40	
.37,	.38	S
.35,	.36	
.33,	.34	J
.31,	.32	
.29,	.30	J
.27,	.28	SS
.25,	.26	JJSSS
.23,	.24	JSS
.21,	.22	JJS
.19,	.20	JSSSS
.17,	.18	SS
.15,	.16	SS
.13,	.14	JSS
.11,	.12	J
.09,	.10	EJJJ
.07,	.08	EEJ
.05,	.06	EEEJS
.03,	.04	
.01,	.02	SS
.00		
-.01,	-.02	E
-.03,	-.04	
-.05,	-.06	EE
-.07,	-.08	J
-.09,	-.10	
-.11,	-.12	E
-.13,	-.14	
-.15,	-.16	J
-.17,	-.18	J
-.19,	-.20	

Note: Correlations are distinguished by grade level: E = Grades 3 to 5; J = Grades 6 to 9; S = Grades 10 to 12.

Figure 3.1. Distribution of Correlations Between Time Spent on Homework and Achievement-Related Outcomes

Is Time Spent On Homework Related to Achievement or Attitudes?

Yes. Forty-three of the 50 correlations indicated that students who reported spending more time on homework also scored higher on a measure of achievement or attitude (the average correlation across the studies was $r = +.19$). Figure 3.1 displays the distribution of the 50 correlations. In Figure 3.1, correlations calculated on elementary, junior high, and high school students are represented by an E, J, or S, respectively.

Does Grade Have an Effect?

Absolutely. In fact, the most dramatic influence on the relationship between time spent on homework and achievement was grade. For high school students (Grades 10 to 12), a sizable average correlation was found ($r = +.25$), whereas for students in Grades 6 to 9, the average correlation was small ($r = +.07$); for elementary school students (Grades 3 to 5), it was nearly nonexistent ($r = +.02$). Figure 3.1 displays this relation by showing the uneven distribution of Es, Js, and Ss across the range of values.

Is Subject Matter Important?

Yes. Mathematics produced the strongest average correlation ($r = +.22$), followed by reading ($r = +.20$) and English ($r = +.20$). Science ($r = +.13$) and social studies ($r = +.10$) produced the smallest average correlations. Examining the order of effects leads to an interesting observation: The average correlations get larger for subjects in which homework assignments are more likely to involve rote learning, practice, or rehearsal. Alternatively, subjects such as science and social studies—which often involve longer term projects, integration of multiple skills, and/or creative use of nonschool resources—show the smallest average correlations. Thinking back to the results described previously, there are now three sets of data suggesting that homework may be more effective for learning simple tasks and one data set suggesting the opposite.

Because significant effects were found for both grade level and subject matter, I wanted to see if the two effects were related. To do so, I calculated average correlations for each subject separately for high school and pre-high school students. As might be expected given previous findings, the effect of subject matter was due entirely to variation among high school students. The pre-high school correlations were all small, and consistently so across subjects.

What About Achievement Versus Attitudes?

A significant relation was also revealed when the type of outcome measure was examined. Although standardized tests ($r = +.18$) and grades ($r = +.19$) produced nearly identical average correlations, the estimate associated with attitudes was smaller ($r = +.14$). This, again, may be due to less trustworthy ways of measuring attitudes and interests than achievement. Or, affective and motivational responses to academic work may be less responsive to homework variations. Finally, teachers may not take a positive attitude into account (as much as high achievement) when they decide how much homework to assign. However, although the difference in average correlations is noteworthy, the magnitude of difference is not great.

Do Student Differences Matter?

Regrettably, I found no evidence on whether the relation between time spent on homework and academic outcomes was influenced by student individual differences. For example, it would be reasonable to expect that some students, perhaps highly academically oriented ones or ones with better study skills, would benefit more from more homework. At this point, however, such assumptions must remain just that, because there is little evidence either to support or to refute such claims.

Does Time Spent on Homework Cause Achievement Differences?

Two types of studies have attempted to address the "causality" question. The first type of study statistically controls variables that might cause *both* time spent on homework and achievement and then looks to see if a relation remains. The second type of study directly manipulates time spent on homework and then measures change in achievement.

I found nine studies that statistically controlled for other variables. The controlled variables ranged from pretest scores to ability measures to gender, race, and economic background to classroom and home conditions. The number of additional variables included in any one analysis ranged from 1 to 16. The results of the nine studies overwhelmingly indicated that the relation between time spent on homework and achievement remains positive and important. However, similar to the results concerning the simple relationship, two of the three studies conducted on students in Grades 4 to 6 yielded predominantly negative results.

In two studies, researchers experimentally varied the amount of homework students were assigned. In one study (Koch, 1965), the amount of homework assigned to three sixth-grade arithmetic classes was determined on a random basis. Conflicting results were found; math concepts favored longer homework assignments and problem solving favored shorter assignments. Another study (Anthony, 1977) involved 18 sections of 9th-, 10th-, and 11th-grade algebra. Each participating teacher taught both one experimental and one control class. A significant effect favoring shorter homework assignments was found.

Taken together then, the two experimental studies lend no support to the notion that longer homework assignments lead to higher achievement, at least in mathematics. This result is especially interesting because math generated the largest estimate of relation among the correlational studies described previously. However, firm conclusions cannot be drawn from two small experiments, especially when they appear to contradict another set of studies that involve many more students, although not in experiments. What is clear is that we cannot rule out the likelihood that at least some of the relationship between time spent on homework and achievement found in surveys is due to higher achievement causing more time spent on homework.

The Curvilinear Relation Between Homework Time and Achievement

In addition to studies that contained data estimating the simple correlation, I found nine studies that reported levels of achievement for different amounts of time spent on homework. The nine studies included a total of 13 independent samples.

By making some considered assumptions, the independent samples could be combined to assess the possibility that there were optimum amounts of homework. Such a relation would be consistent with results in related areas. For instance, the relationship between time spent on the task and achievement seems to reach a plateau at which increases in time have only a marginal effect on

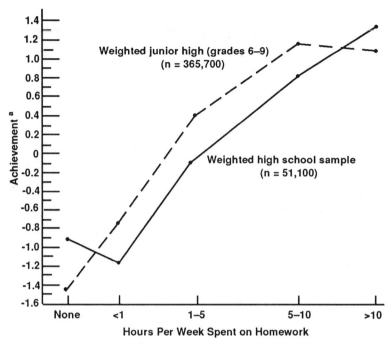

Note: [a] Scale is based on standardized, within-study mean achievement for each level of homework.

Figure 3.2. Analysis of the Curvilinear Relation Between Homework Time and Achievement

learning (Fredrick & Walberg, 1980). This could also be the case with time on homework.

Is There an Optimum Amount of Homework?

Apparently so. But again, it differs from grade to grade. Figure 3.2 presents the results of the analysis for junior high and high school students. It reveals that for high school students the positive relation between homework time and achievement does not appear until at least 1 hour of homework per week is reported. Then it continues to climb unabated to the highest measured interval (more than 2 hours). In contrast, for junior high students the positive relation appears for even the most minimal level of time spent on homework (less than 1 hour) but disappears entirely at the highest interval. Only one study was available for Grades 1 to 6 (Hinckley, 1979). It seemed unwise to draw any conclusions about possible curvilinear relations for elementary school students based on a single study.

What About Causality?

Again, because the results are correlational, a causal interpretation of these data can be framed in different ways. For example, it is possible that achievement causes time on homework. If this is the case, then teachers of junior high students might be advised to use achievement as a guide for how much homework to assign for all students except the brightest in the class. Distinctions in amount of homework would not be made among the brightest students, at least not based on achievement differences. For high school students, teachers would not use achievement as a basis for assigning homework to lower achievers, but achievement becomes a causal factor as performance improves.

Another way to construe these data is to view homework as the cause of achievement. When this approach is taken, the data have important implications for homework policies. That is, Figure 3.2 indicates that small amounts of homework for high school students are of little utility. However, once a critical amount is reached, perhaps about 1 hour per week, increases in time spent on homework, up to more than 10 hours per week, cause improvement in achievement. No data are available beyond this point. For junior high students, even less than 1 hour of homework a week might improve achievement, until between 5 and 10 hours per week are assigned. At this point, there appears to be no advantage to increases in time spent on homework.

Summary

In sum, 50 correlations based on over 112,000 students revealed a positive relation between student reports of time spent on homework and several academic outcomes. However, it is still plausible, based on these data alone, that teachers assign more homework to students achieving better or that better students spend more time on home study. In studies where third variables were controlled, the positive relation remained for older students but was not evident before high school. Also, the magnitude of the relation appears to be modified by the outcome measure, the subject, and, especially, the grade of the student.

Finally, the relation between homework and achievement reached a point of diminishing returns for junior high school students but not for high school students. If homework is taken as the causal agent, the results suggest that increases in time spent on home study have more of a positive effect on the achievement of students at higher grades. Increasing the amount of homework for middle-grade students may be efficacious only up to a certain point. There is no evidence that any amount of homework noticeably improves the academic performance of elementary students.

Variations in the
Homework Process

In this chapter, three types of variations in assignments are examined that might be related to the value of homework. First, the content of assignments is considered. The questions asked involve (a) whether the content of homework should appear before, after, or concurrently with its discussion in class; (b) whether teachers should individualize homework within classes; and (c) whether homework assignments are better if they are voluntary or required. Next, the role of parents and the community in the homework process is discussed. Specifically, the role of community-based homework hot lines is examined. Finally, I turn my attention to different forms of teacher feedback and incentives after assignments are turned in.

Content of Assignments

Is the Temporal Relation of Classwork and Homework Important?

Yes. I found eight studies that examined whether the amount of dispersion of content across homework assignments influences homework's effectiveness. "Same-day-content" homework requires students to work on problems that pertain only to material presented in class on the day the problems are assigned. "Distributed" homework assignments include the introduction of material that has not yet been covered in class and/or that was covered in lessons before the current day. In terms of the instructional purposes detailed in chapter 1, distributed strategies that include material not yet covered are meant to prepare students for upcoming topics, whereas coverage of previous material is meant as practice or review.

Several studies included measures of the effect of the different strategies, not only immediately after the classroom unit was completed but also when a delay occurred between the end of the unit and testing. This permitted an assessment of the strategies in terms of both short- and long-term retention.

All seven studies that included tests of achievement given immediately after the unit revealed positive effects of distributed homework over same-day-content homework. The average student who did preparation, practice, or both types of distributed homework outperformed 54% of students who did only same-day-content homework.

Two studies comparing preparation homework with current-content homework revealed larger differences than the three studies comparing practice and current-content homework. This result gives some indication that preparation homework may be more effective than practice homework in increasing students' scores on immediate measures of achievement.

The five studies that included measures of achievement taken sometime after a unit was completed also uniformly indicated that distributed homework was more effective than same-day-content homework. The average student in the distributed-homework classrooms scored higher on the delayed measures of achievement than did 57% of students in the same-day-content homework classrooms. The one delayed-measurement study that examined a treatment including both preparation and practice homework revealed a larger effect than did the four studies that examined one or the other instructional purpose.

The two studies that included preparation homework only did not differ in effect from three studies that included practice homework only, although a trend did, again, indicate that preparation homework may be more effective than practice homework.

As a whole, the studies of content timing are trustworthy (e.g., treatments were randomly assigned to classes, and students were apparently assigned to classes without bias). However, certain precautions need to be taken in the generalization of these findings. First, no study has examined the effect of the timing of homework on students in elementary school. Also, mathematics was the predominant subject of instruction.

Do Student Differences Affect Preparation or Practice Homework?

I could find none. Four studies that examined whether the effect of preparation and/or practice homework on achievement was moderated by the intelligence of students revealed no noteworthy difference. Similar results were reported in a study involving student gender and a study in which teachers rated students on their "dependence proneness."

What About Attitudes?

The two studies that included a measure of student attitudes produced negligible effects. It appears that the temporal relation between homework and classwork has little effect on students' attitudes toward the covered material.

Should Teachers Individualize Assignments Within a Class?

Generally, no—at least not without good reasons associated with particular students or classes. Whether individualizing homework for students at different performance levels improves achievement has been the topic of four studies. Taken together, the studies revealed no consistent improvement in achievement when classes with individualized homework were compared to classes in which all students did the same assignment. Two well-conducted studies indicated that the effect of individualization was influenced by numerous other factors, and not necessarily the same, or even consistent, ones. One researcher (Bradley, 1967) compared not only achievement but the amount of time both students and teachers spent on homework when it was and was not individualized. The results indicated that slower students required more time to complete non-individualized homework and that teachers spent considerably more time constructing and monitoring individualized assignments.

Thus past research hints at individualization being effective for some subjects and with certain subgroups of students. Further, logic dictates that individualization would be appropriate in some circumstances; for instance, when classes contain heterogeneous students. However, individualization of homework does not reveal benefits widespread enough to suggest it be adopted as a matter of general policy. In addition, individualization may significantly increase the time teachers spend preparing and correcting assignments.

Should Homework Be Compulsory or Voluntary?

In the past 40 years, only one study has compared the effects of compulsory versus voluntary homework. This small study (involving 113 students) found no differences in achievement between the two approaches.

Clearly, however, one can think of circumstances involving high-interest homework where more academic change might be produced if the assignment were voluntary than if it were required. This reasoning rests on the assumption that, if children do things without the presence of obvious external demands, they are more likely to internalize positive sentiments about the activity (cf. Deci & Ryan, 1985). One can also think of circumstances where voluntary assignments would go undone, making requirement essential for any learning to take place. It would be imprudent, therefore, to conclude that the two practices had equal effect until larger and more varied studies are conducted.

Home and Community Factors

In Table 1.3, three home or community factors were identified that might influence the utility of homework: leisure activity competitors for student time, home environment conditions that either facilitate or inhibit students' opportunities to study, and the involvement of others. Of these, only the involvement of parents in the homework process has been the subject of research. There is also a large and growing research literature that looks at family literacy in general and at the family as a source of informal education. Although these issues are considerably broader than homework, a short description of some related research will be given. Also, several communities have instituted programs that provide after-school telephone assistance to students with homework problems. These programs have never been formally evaluated for their influence on achievement, but a description of one such program is in order.

Should Parents Have a Formal Role in Homework?

In six recent studies, the relation between parent involvement in homework and achievement has been examined. Five of these studies were correlational in design, and one involved an experimental manipulation. The five correlational studies produced three results showing that more parent involvement was associated with higher achievement and two results showing that more involvement was related to lower achievement, with the latter results appearing in more recent studies.

Again, the interpretation of these correlational findings is complicated by our inability to infer causality in such studies. That is, these correlations can be interpreted to mean that involvement causes achievement, achievement causes involvement, neither, or both. For instance, a negative relation might indicate that parent involvement interferes with learning, if involvement causes learning. Alternatively, it could mean that parents of students who are doing poorly in school may be asked more often, or may volunteer, to get more involved in homework, if achievement causes involvement.

The only study that attempted to manipulate directly the presence or absence of parent involvement showed no effects on the primary achievement measures employed. However, this study had several design flaws and only a small sample of students and classrooms. Thus, although parent involvement in homework has received more attention than other related topics, the generally low trustworthiness of the studies makes it unwise to draw any conclusions about the strategy's effectiveness.

Does this mean families have no role in education? Of course not. The studies described above related to the narrow circumstance in which parents take an active role in helping a child complete homework. There is a burgeoning line of more general inquiry examining how families act as educators. Much of the associated research involves observation of children in the home, often when they are doing homework, assisted or not. The observations focus on physical arrangements, time patterns, and attention paid to procedural matters. Researchers look for how families integrate homework into the flow of daily events and how they move between homework and other social activities.

Also, there is a large and growing literature relating to how parents can become involved in schools beyond simply assisting with homework (Epstein, 1987a, 1987b) and how parents can be trained to be better transmitters of knowledge (e.g., Levenstein, 1983).

Do Homework Hot Lines Help?

One type of community-based effort related to homework involves the establishment of homework "hot lines." These are telephone services in which teachers are available to answer questions related to homework problems. One notable effort was the Dial-A-Teacher Program instituted by the school district of Philadelphia (Blackwell, 1979). The idea behind the service was to help callers who did not have available at home the resources necessary to solve problems encountered in homework or who might have forgotten the procedure needed to complete an assignment.

It is difficult to assess the effectiveness of such programs using the outcome variables that appear in other types of homework research. However, logic suggests that in some school districts, especially large ones, the hot lines might be of some service while being run in a cost-effective manner.

Teacher Feedback and Incentives

The response of teachers when homework assignments are brought back to school can vary in four ways. First, teachers can provide students with instruction on how the assignment could have been completed more accurately. This can be done by reviewing all or a portion of the assigned work with the class as a whole or by providing individual students with written comments describing their errors. Second, teachers can provide letter or numerical grades. These grades can then be used as part of the student's overall performance evaluation. Third, teachers can give praise or criticism, either verbal or written, meant to reward correct responses and/or punish incorrect ones. Both grades and reinforcement can be based simply on whether the homework was completed or on the accuracy of the responses. Finally, teachers can provide nonverbal incentives, such as candy or early dismissal, dependent on the completeness or accuracy of the homework. The four strategies can be applied in combination and with varying frequencies, ranging from continuous to intermittent use of any given strategy.

Are Comments and Grading Important to the Utility of Homework?

Surprisingly, I found no study that tested whether the presence versus the absence of a feedback strategy influenced the value of homework. Apparently, educators believe that the value of such strategies is so obvious that testing is unnecessary.

A few studies have involved comparing different strategies to one another. Two studies examined the effects of different types of instructional comments (that is, simply telling students an answer was wrong versus describing the type of error). Neither study found a reliable difference. One study looked at performance differences between classes that discussed all homework questions versus classes that went over only questions requested by the students. No differences between the strategies were found. Two studies of evaluative comments (praise and/or critical remarks versus no feedback) also showed no effect on the value of homework for improving achievement. Finally, three studies of grading strategies—one comparing grading every math problem versus grading only a random sample and two comparing grading for completeness versus grading for accuracy—also produced no differences.

What About Providing Incentives?

Studies of the effects of incentives suggest that provision of rewards for handing in homework can increase completion rates. The types of rewards employed have included extra play time on computers, extra free time, coupons for purchases at the school store, and "free homework" passes that allow students to skip future assignments without penalty. It is no surprise that most of these studies have focused on students with learning disabilities or poor motivation.

Summary

In sum then, the eight studies examining practice and preparation homework provide a convincing, consistent pattern favoring these assignment purposes. In fact, distributed assignments had a larger impact on delayed than immediate measurement of achievement, meaning they may be especially important for promoting retention of material.

Research on variations in feedback strategies reveals little reason to choose one strategy over another. Whether or how much instructional feedback is given, whether all or only some problems are graded, and whether the teacher provides evaluative comments appear to have little relation to homework's effectiveness for improving performance. There is sound evidence that providing incentives for completion to students who are disadvantaged or learning disabled proves beneficial.

Homework Policy Guidelines

In this chapter, I examine homework policy guidelines that have been developed by national organizations, with particular attention to aspects of the policies that are and are not supported by empirical evidence. I conclude the chapter with a set of generic policies based on the findings of my own review.

Policy Guides From National Organizations

What Works

The most popular publication ever printed by the U.S. government is a booklet entitled *What Works* (U.S. Department of Education, 1986). This booklet was intended to be a distillation of research on teaching and learning. Not surprisingly, it contains sections that relate to both the quantity and quality of homework assignments. Figure 5.1 reproduces the section on homework quantity in *What Works*.

Based on my findings, there is a major qualifier to the assertion in *What Works* that amount of homework and student achievement are positively related—it applies only to high school students. The graphs in Figure 5.1 portray a linear relation between amount of

Percent Correct

**Test Scores of 1982 Seniors in
Reading, Science, and Mathematics
by Amount of Homework per Week**

**Student achievement rises significantly when teachers regularly
assign homework and students consciously do it.**

Extra studying helps children at all levels of ability. One research
study reveals that when low–ability students do just 1 to 3 hours of
homework a week, their grades are usually as high as those of
average–ability students who do not do homework. Similarly, when
average–ability students do 3 to 5 hours of homework a week, their
grades usually equal those of high–ability students who do no
homework.

Homework boosts achievement because the total time spent
studying influences how much is learned. Low–achieving high school
students study less than high achievers and do less homework. Time
is not the only ingredient of learning, but without it little can be
achieved.

Teachers, parents, and students determine how much, how useful ,
and how good the homework is. On average, American teachers say
they assign about 10 hours of homework each week–about 2 hours
per school day. But high school seniors report they spend only 4 to 5
hours a week doing homework, and 10 percent say they do none at
all or have none assigned. In contrast, students in Japan spend
about twice as much time studying outside school as American
students.

References: Coleman, J.S., Hoffer, T., and Kilgore, S. (1982) *High School Achievement:
Public, Catholic and Private Schools Compared.* New York: Basic Books.

Keith, T.Z. (April 1982). "Time Spent on Homework and High School Grades: A
Large-Sample Path Analysis." *Journal of Educational Psychology,* Vol. 74, No.
2, pp. 248–253.

National Center for Education Statistics. (April 1983). *School District Survey of
Academic Requirements and Achievement.* Washington, D.C.: U.S. Department
of Education, Fast Response Survey Systems. ERIC Document No. ED 238097.

Rohlen, T.P. (1983). *Japan's High Schools.* Berkley, CA: University of California
Press.

Walberg, H.J. (1984) "Improving the Productivity of America's Schools."
Educational Leadership, Vol. 41, No. 8, pp. 19–36.

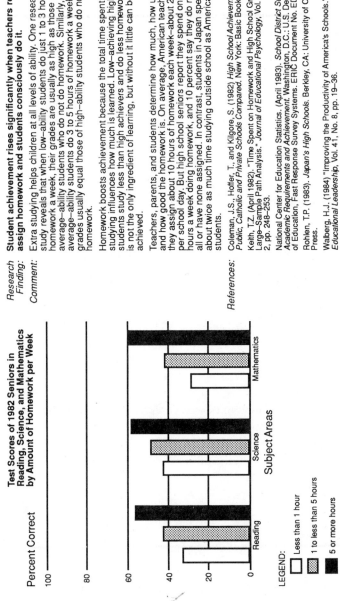

Figure 5.1. "What Works" on Homework Quantity

homework per week and achievement scores. My review showed that junior high school students doing 5 to 10 hours of homework a week performed no better on achievement tests than did students doing 1 to 5 hours of homework. In Grades 4 to 6 there was no meaningful relation between time on homework and achievement. No data exist for lower level elementary school grades.

The comments in Figure 5.1 seem justifiable. The first paragraph contains an easily understood description of homework's effect size (based, however, on results of a single study). The next paragraph includes a reasonable theoretical rationale for the homework-achievement link. The third paragraph points out that teachers report assigning more homework than students report doing. In the context of high schools, the comments are sound. If applied to other grades, they may be misleading.

Figure 5.2 contains the section in *What Works* on the quality of homework. The paragraph on the research findings suffers from a vagueness in the description of homework's effect. No outcome measure is mentioned for gauging the influence of well-designed—that is, carefully prepared, thoroughly explained, and promptly commented on—homework. The comment is more specific. However, my review of research indicates that only one outcome appears to have withstood empirical testing—well-designed homework is more likely to be completed than is homework that is not well designed. The nonacademic effects cited in the second and third paragraphs have never been the focus of research.

The authors of *What Works* carefully avoid making assertions about the effect of well-designed homework on achievement. Of the several components of well-designed homework, only comments and criticisms have been tested for their influence on test scores. However, in these studies researchers examined different feedback strategies rather than the presence versus absence of feedback per se.

Kappa Delta Pi

Kappa Delta Pi, the international honor society in education, publishes a series of booklets on classroom practices. One booklet, authored by Timothy Keith (1986), includes a discussion of homework. The issues Keith focuses on are time, grade level, subject matter, quality, individualization, parent involvement, and feed-

Research Finding

Well-designed homework assignments relate directly to classwork and extend students' learning beyond the classroom. Homework is most useful when teachers carefully prepare the assignment, thoroughly explain it, and give prompt comments and criticism when the work is completed.

Comment

To make the most of what students learn from doing homework, teachers need to give the same care to preparing homework assignments as they give to classroom instruction. When teachers prepare written instructions and discuss homework assignments with students, they find their students take the homework more seriously than if the assignments are simply announced. Students are more willing to do homework when they believe it is useful, when teachers treat it as an integral part of instruction, when it is evaluated by the teacher, and when it counts as a part of the grade.

Assignments that require students to think, and are therefore more interesting, foster their desire to learn both in and out of school. Such activities include explaining what is seen or read in class; comparing, relating and experimenting with ideas; and analyzing principles.

Effective homework assignments do not just supplement the classroom lesson; they also teach students to be independent learners. Homework gives students experience in following directions, making judgments and comparisons, raising additional questions for study, and developing responsibility and self-discipline.

References

Austin, J. (1976). "Do Comments on Mathematics Homework Affect Student Achievement?" *School Science and Mathematics*, Vol. 76, No. 2, pp. 159–164.

Coulter, F. (1980). "Secondary School Homework: Cooperative Research Study Report No. 7." ERIC Document No. ED 209200.

Dick, D. (1980). "An Experimental Study of the Effects of Required Homework Review Versus Review on Request Upon Achievement. " ERIC Document No. ED 194320.

Featherstone, H. (February 1985). "Homework." *The Harvard Education Letter.*

Walberg, H.J. (April 1985). "Homework's Powerful Effects on Learning." *Educational Leadership.* Vol. 42, No. 7, pp.76–79.

Figure 5.2. "What Works" on Homework Quality

back. Exhibit 5.1 presents excerpts on each of these topics from Keith's work.

Keith's general recommendations regarding time students should spend on homework reflect the research finding that homework is

EXHIBIT 5.1 Excerpts From Keith (1986) on Issues in Homework

Time

Much will depend on the individual community, the individual school teacher, and even the individual student. Nevertheless, the following time ranges, geared toward the average student, should be workable for many situations.

Ten to 45 minutes per night in Grades 1 to 3.

Forty-five to 90 minutes per night in Grades 4 to 6.

One to 2 hours per night for Grades 7 through 9.

Ninety minutes to 2 1/2 hours per night for Grades 10 through 12.

Grade level

Types of homework assigned should change, at least in proportion, as children grow older. If the types of homework are considered a hierarchy, from practice at the lowest level to creative at the highest, it seems apparent that, in general, the proportion of higher level homework should increase with grade level.

Subject matter

Math and Spelling, for example, lend themselves to practice assignments, especially in the early grades, while a class in Literature would seem to lend itself to preparation and creative homework. But again, there is much room for variation, depending on the purpose, the particular topic being covered, and the grade level of the students.

Quality

The purposes of the assignment should be clear, to the teacher and to the students, as should the notion of how the students should profit and what they should learn from the assignment. The tasks assigned should be relevant to what the children are learning in school, and the assignment type should be appropriate for the purposes, the grade, and the subject matter. Finally, there should be some review or reinforcement of assignments so that homework is not a dead end. If the tasks assigned as homework have a worthwhile purpose in the first place, they should certainly be worth following up in class.

It is often wise to start a homework assignment in class in order to make sure students understand the assignment and are getting off on the right foot. This practice will be especially important for less able students or when students in the class are completing different assignments.

EXHIBIT 5.1 Continued

Individualization

In many cases, homework may offer an opportunity to provide some differential, or individualized, instruction. This does not mean that every child in the class needs a different homework assignment every night. On the other hand, it is quite possible to vary the difficulty level, and at times even the assignment type, for those students in the class who seem unlikely to benefit from the assignment as given.

Parent involvement

The wisest course would seem to be to keep parental involvement to a minimum (Rosemond, 1984). Parents should provide a quiet place for their children to study, even if only the kitchen table. They should provide the structure and the encouragement to help the child complete the assignment, and they should convey that they feel the completion of homework (and learning in general) is important. . . . Parents should also be available to help with an occasional question if they feel comfortable in this role, and they should be available to review completed assignments if there is time (Rosemond, 1984).

Again, while extensive involvement may be helpful on occasion, minimal involvement in actual homework should be the rule; parents should be encouraged to remember that it is their *child's* homework, not theirs. . . . As with any rule, there are exceptions. And the parental involvement rule should probably be relaxed with elementary students.

Feedback

Once students have completed homework, their work should be evaluated in some way. This generally means collecting, evaluating, and returning their assignments. . . . Although not every assignment must be graded, it is good to remember that homework that is graded or commented on seems to produce higher achievement than homework that is ungraded (Paschal et al., 1984). Thus graded homework should be the norm. . . . Comments, particularly *positive* comments, on students' papers will also produce better learning (cf., Austin, 1976; Page, 1958; Paschal et al., 1984), as well as demonstrating that you think homework is important.

Source: From *Homework* by T. Z. Keith, 1986, West Lafayette, IN: Kappa Delta Pi. Copyright 1986 by Kappa Delta Pi. Reprinted by permission.

more efficacious at higher grades. However, the results of my review are somewhat at odds with his time recommendations, especially for upper elementary and junior high school students. Considering the generally small effects of homework on achievement in fourth through sixth grade, an upper range of 90 minutes of homework per night as Keith suggests seems excessive. Likewise, the data indicate that students in seventh through ninth grade doing 1 hour of homework per night perform as well as students doing closer to 2 hours. Bear in mind as well that the estimates of time spent on homework were generally provided by the students themselves and are therefore more likely to be over- than underestimates. In general, then, my recommendation is that Keith's lower ranges should actually serve as guidelines for the average amount of homework teachers should assign per night at each grade level.

If homework has no noticeable effect on achievement in elementary school grades, why assign any at all? Keith's comments on grade level and parent involvement hint at what I think is the primary rationale. In earlier grades, students can be given homework assignments meant not so much to foster achievement as to promote good attitudes and study habits, to dispel the notion that learning occurs only in school, and to allow parents the opportunity to express to their children how much they value education. In order for such effects to occur, it seems crucial that assignments be short and simple. Of course, there is as yet no research evidence to support or to refute whether the recommended types of homework for elementary schoolchildren actually have the intended effects.

With regard to subject matter, Keith points out the subtle differences in content that may lie behind the fact that homework is differentially effective for different subjects. He suggests that math and spelling lend themselves to practice assignments. My review found that subjects and topics amenable to practice- and preparation-type assignments also showed the strongest relation between homework and achievement. Based on this reasoning, I suggested that homework may be most effective for the learning of simple tasks. However, if the purpose of homework is to generate interest in a topic, assignments should be more challenging, requiring the use of higher order thinking skills and the integration of different domains of knowledge.

The main message of my review of homework research regarding both grade level and content is clear. Teachers should not assign homework to young children with the expectation that it will noticeably enhance achievement. Nor should they expect students to be capable of teaching themselves complex skills at home. Instead, teachers might assign short and simple homework to younger students, hoping it will foster positive, long-term, education-related behaviors and attitudes. Simple assignments should be given to older students to improve achievement and complex assignments to generate interest in the subject matter.

Keith's recommendations regarding quality mirror those made in *What Works*. Again, the suggestions make good sense, although a research base for them is lacking. Keith also neglects to mention the value of distributing the content of homework across multiple assignments.

Although Keith's recommendation concerning individualization seems innocuous, teachers should not expect great benefits to accrue from the practice. My sense is that individualized homework for students in the same class will rarely prove more effective than well-constructed group or class assignments. This statement is based on the assumption that most classrooms have relatively homogeneous student bodies. To the extent that learning skills are not homogeneous, individualization might take on some added value. In earlier grades, assignments should be short and simple enough so that they pose no great difficulty to any student, although the time required to complete them may vary. In higher grades, choice in class selection usually produces more homogeneous groups of students, but the groups may differ, on average. In such cases, different homework assignments for various classes are certainly called for. Furthermore, if teachers teach, for example, one average and one accelerated class, they might consider having the brightest students in the average class do parts of the homework assigned to the accelerated group.

I find myself in complete agreement with Keith's suggestions concerning parent involvement. Research examining whether there are positive effects to casting parents formally in the role of teacher is inconclusive. Considering the claimed positive and negative effects, it may be best for teachers not to promote too much direct involvement by parents. However, it makes good sense to have parents play a supportive role in the homework process. Indeed, some facilitation from parents is probably necessary for successful learning through homework. Teachers should encourage parents to take part in supportive but indirect ways.

Finally, Keith's recommendations (and those of many others) concerning evaluation of homework are not based on research findings. My review found no studies of the effects of grading or evaluative comments versus no grading or comments on the effectiveness of homework. The existing research indicates that different strategies for providing feedback differ little in their influence on homework. Realistically, it seems that students might not take assignments seriously or might not complete them at all if students are not going to be monitored, either through grading or some penalty for failure to turn in the work. The evidence suggests, however, that intermittent grading and comments are no less effective than providing continuous feedback. I suggest, therefore, that the practice of grading homework be kept to a minimum, especially if the assignment's purpose is to foster positive attitudes toward the subject matter. Grading might provide external reasons for doing homework that detract from students' appreciation of the intrinsic value of the exercise.

This does not mean that homework assignments should go unmonitored. All homework should be collected and teachers should use it in the diagnosis of learning difficulties. If a teacher notices a student falling behind in class, homework assignments can be carefully scrutinized to determine where the difficulty lies. When errors or misunderstandings on homework are found, the teacher should more assiduously go over the student's other assignments. Problems can then be communicated directly to the student. In a sense, then, homework can help teachers individualize instruction. I see no more reason to treat each homework assignment as if it were a test than I see reason to grade students for their performance on each class lesson.

In sum, I generally agree with Keith's homework guidelines, with four exceptions. First, his ranges for appropriate amounts of time spent on homework may be too long. I suggest that his lower range serve as an average. Second, I would be more explicit about the different purposes of homework for students in different grades.

Third, Keith omits the distribution of content across assignments as a key element of quality homework. Fourth, Keith endorses the use of grading and evaluative comments on homework assignments. I am more equivocal. I view homework more as a diagnostic device than an opportunity to test. Furthermore, the grading of homework may severely limit its ability to foster positive attitudes toward the material.

Phi Delta Kappa

The Phi Delta Kappa Educational Foundation publishes a series of booklets called "fastbacks" that are meant to promote a better understanding of schooling. One fastback is on homework. Its authors, David England and Joannis Flatley (1985), base their recommendations partly on research and partly on conversations about homework that they had with parents, principals, teachers, and students. England and Flatley's suggestions are summarized in a section of their fastback entitled "Homework Do's and Don'ts." These are reproduced in Exhibit 5.2.

England and Flatley focus primarily on the interpersonal aspects of homework—what should be expected of the different participants in the process and how expectations need to be communicated. These nicely complement the more substantive recommendations contained in Keith (1986).

Perhaps the most noteworthy aspect of England and Flatley's (1985) discussion is its skepticism about the value of too much compulsory homework. They write:

> Then, too, kids need time to be kids—which is more than a kid's argument. . . . Just getting kids to do homework becomes recurring ground for battle in many homes. In the background we hear chants of "Teach them discipline!" and "They must learn life is demanding!" We would submit that taking a cold shower teaches discipline, too; and, compared to doing homework until 11:00 p.m. three or four nights a week, it would probably do more to keep kids awake in school. As for learning that life is demanding, perhaps being in school seven hours a day is demanding enough. And if it is not, having the school day encroach on what might otherwise be family time may not be the solution. (pp. 11-12)

EXHIBIT 5.2 England and Flatley's (1985) Homework Do's and Don'ts

The following homework do's and don'ts provide a quick summary of the points covered in the preceding narrative. Our lists are selective but not mutually exclusive. We have tried to limit our admonitions to those few we feel would really matter if heeded.

For principals

1. *Do not* believe everything you hear about a teacher's homework practices.
2. *Do not* expect all teachers to be equally enthusiastic about a school-wide homework policy.
3. *Do not* expect a schoolwide policy to please all parents.
4. *Do not* expect teachers with the heaviest instructional loads to assign as much homework as those with the lightest loads.
5. *Do* check out all rumors that come your way about teachers' homework practices.
6. *Do* put the teachers you least expect to be pleased by a schoolwide homework policy on the committee that formulates it.
7. *Do* involve parents in the development of schoolwide homework policies.
8. *Do* everything possible to assist teachers with managing homework paper loads, including use of school aides and parent volunteers.

For teachers

1. *Do not* ever give homework as punishment.
2. *Do not* make up spur-of-the-moment homework assignments.
3. *Do not* assume that because there are no questions asked about a homework assignment that students have no questions about the assignment.
4. *Do not* expect students (even your best students) always to have their homework assignments completed.
5. *Do* understand that not all types of homework assignments are equally valuable for all types of students.
6. *Do* explain the specific purpose of every homework assignment.
7. *Do* listen to what students say about their experiences in completing your homework assignments.
8. *Do* acknowledge and be thankful for efforts students make to complete their homework.

For parents

1. *Do* make sure your child really needs help before offering to help with homework.

EXHIBIT 5.2 Continued

2. *Do* help your child see a purpose or some value in homework assignments.
3. *Do* encourage your children to complete assignments after absences from school.
4. *Do* suggest an alternative to watching TV on nights when no homework is assigned, such as sharing a magazine article, enjoying a game together, or going to an exhibit or concert.
5. *Do not* try to help with homework if you are confused and really cannot figure out what is expected.
6. *Do not* hesitate to have your child explain legitimate reasons for nights when homework simply cannot be completed.
7. *Do not* place yourself in an adversarial role between your child and teachers over homework issues until all other alternatives are exhausted.
8. *Do not* feel your child always has to be doing "something productive." (There are few things sadder than a burned-out 14-year-old.)

For students

1. *Do* ask your parents for help with your homework only when you really need help.
2. *Do* ask the teacher for help before or after class if you are confused about a homework assignment.
3. *Do* explain to teachers legitimate reasons that sometimes make it impossible to complete some homework assignments.
4. *Do* make every effort to complete homework assignments when they are very important for a particular class.
5. *Do not* expect that your parents will be able to help with all your homework. (Parents forget things they have learned, and some of what is taught in school today is foreign to adults.)
6. *Do not* ask teachers to help with any homework assignments you really can complete independently.
7. *Do not* confuse *excuses* for incomplete homework assignments with legitimate *reasons.*
8. *Do not* think doing your homework "most of the time" will be satisfactory for those classes where homework counts the most. (In such classes, even a 75% completion rate may not be enough.)

England and Flatley are not against homework, but they do see problems in its implementation. One of their major concerns is captured nicely in their fourth admonition to teachers: "Do not expect students (even your best students) always to have their homework assignments completed." This raises two questions: Should homework be mandatory, and if so, what should be the consequence for failure to complete assignments?

I believe that most homework should be compulsory. The kinds of difficulties that England and Flatley describe should not arise if assignments are kept to a reasonable length. Voluntary homework should also be assigned on occasion. It might be reserved for assignments that students will find most interesting, because voluntary assignments are probably most valuable for producing intrinsic motivation.

Consistent with the feedback policy outlined above, I recommend that formal sanctions be associated with uncompleted homework assignments only in serious cases of neglect. Again, missing assignments should be viewed as diagnostic and treated in the context of the student's overall learning performance. Although some positive or negative incentive may be necessary, it should be kept to a minimum, again so as not to interfere with what should be the obvious intrinsic merits of completing assignments. It seems doctrinaire to reduce the grade of an otherwise straight-A student for assignments not completed. Likewise, missing assignments of poor-performing students are more likely symptom than cause.

Other Sources of Policy Guidelines

The three policy guides I have examined include the major issues that need to be addressed when a district, a school, or a teacher decides to develop a policy on homework. The national organization guides, however, are by no means exhaustive. Other excellent sources of information also exist.

The Pennsylvania Department of Education (1984) published a resource folder entitled *Homework Policies and Guidelines*. Its authors take the position that a clearly written policy is necessary for homework to be effective. The resource folder contains guidelines for preparing homework policies, suggestions about factors to be considered for inclusion in policies, and, most important, examples of district policies. The examples range from quite brief to remarkably detailed.

The Connecticut Department of Education (1984) published a manual on policy development and administrative procedures entitled *Attendance, Homework, Promotion and Retention*. The manual is composed from policies and procedures submitted by 96 Connecticut school districts. A panel of school administrators and teachers then isolated key policy elements and identified good examples of policies and procedures. The manual contains many sample policies but does not evaluate their content.

Similar although less ambitious manuals have been developed by state agencies in Indiana, Kentucky, and Minnesota. I am certain that other states have also undertaken the task of helping school districts develop homework policies.

Finally, examples of homework policies are obtainable from school districts and even individual schools. From the letters I received while conducting my review, it was obvious that many schools and districts take great pride in the care and thoroughness with which their policies have been constructed.

Guidelines Based on the Present Review

It is advisable that homework policies exist at the district, school, and classroom levels. The issues addressed at each level are generally different, although some overlap.

District Policies

At the district level, the detail of a policy need not be great, but the policy should address the general purposes of homework. A policy should at least contain a succinct statement indicating that homework is a cost-effective instructional technique that should have a positive effect on student achievement. The policy should also state that homework may also have some unique benefits for the general character development of children. Finally, homework may serve as a vital link between schools, families, and the broader community.

It is also important that district policies address three substantive issues. These guides would be meant to prevent the wide variations in practices from one school to another that so often cause trouble for administrators and teachers. However, the recommendations should be broad enough so that schools have ample flexibility to respond to local conditions.

First, my recommendation is that districts adopt a policy that requires some homework to be assigned at all grade levels but recognizes that a mixture of both mandatory and voluntary assignments may be most beneficial to students.

Second, districts should prescribe general ranges for the frequency and duration of assignments. These ought to reflect the grade-level differences mentioned previously but should also be influenced by community factors. Such guidelines for a nationally representative, or generic, district might be the following:

- Grades 1 to 3: one to three mandatory assignments per week, each lasting no more than 15 minutes
- Grades 4 to 6: two to four mandatory assignments per week, each lasting between 15 and 45 minutes
- Grades 7 to 9: three to five mandatory assignments per week, each lasting (in total) between 45 and 75 minutes
- Grades 10 to 12: four to five mandatory assignments per week, each lasting (in total) between 75 and 120 minutes

Third, district policies need to acknowledge that homework should serve different purposes at varying grades. For younger students, homework should be used to foster positive attitudes toward school and better academic-related behaviors and character traits, not primarily to improve subject matter achievement. As students grow older, the function of homework should gradually change toward facilitating the acquisition of knowledge in specific topics.

School Policies

A school homework policy might further specify the time ranges for different grade levels and subjects. This is especially important in schools where different subjects are taught by different teachers. A scheme must be adopted so that each teacher knows (a) what days of the week are available to him or her for homework assignments and (b) how much of the students' total daily homework time is allocated to that subject. School policies should also contain guidelines that describe the roles of administrators in the homework process. Communicating the district and school policy to parents, monitoring the implementation of the policy, and coordinating the scheduling of homework among different teachers, if needed, should be included in the administrative guidelines.

Whether or not guidelines for teachers should be included in schoolwide homework policies is a decision best made at each school. Some teachers might view such policies as unnecessary intrusions on their professional judgment. Others might perceive them as opportunities to learn from the experience of other teachers and to foster a strong community spirit in the school.

I recommend that schoolwide policies relating to the role of the teacher focus primarily on the design of high-quality assignments. Among these recommendations would be that teachers clearly state (a) how the assignment is related to the topic under study, (b) the purpose of the assignment, (c) how the assignment might best be carried out, and (d) what the student needs to do to demonstrate that the assignment has been completed. It is also important that teachers ensure that students have available the necessary resources to carry out an assignment.

Classroom Policies

Finally, teachers need to adopt a policy governing homework in their classes. A nationally representative classroom might adopt the following classroom policies:

- Assignments will generally be the same for all students in the class or learning group. Although individualization may occur, it will be the exception rather than the rule.
- Students are expected to complete all mandatory homework assignments. Failure to do so will necessitate remedial activities.
- Individualization and choice in homework will be obtained through the provision of voluntary assignments of high interest to students.
- The teacher will not formally evaluate or grade each homework assignment.

Although it would be ideal for all assignments to be carefully scrutinized, time constraints might not make this possible. Teachers should at least scan students' work to get a sense of whether they have taken the assignment seriously. If homework indicates that a student does not understand the concepts or has not mastered the skills, it should be used to help guide interactive instruction between the teacher and the student.

- Homework assignments will disperse content so that topics will appear in assignments before and after they are covered in class.
- Homework will not be used to teach complex skills and material. If the purpose of homework is to enhance achievement, it will generally focus on the learning of simple skills and material. More complex tasks (e.g., writing compositions or research reports) can be valuable assignments but should generally require the integration of skills students already possess.
- Parents will rarely be asked to assist in homework in a formal instructional role. Instead, their help will be recruited to ensure that the home environment facilitates student self-study.

These guidelines, along with others, should be explicitly communicated to students and parents. "Do's and Don'ts" lists like those suggested by England and Flatley (1985) are a useful format for conveying homework rules and roles.

As I have stated in numerous previous contexts, the general guidelines I offer are not applicable to all classrooms. They need to be adapted to meet local conditions. They also must be supplemented with recommendations concerning other aspects of homework, for example, the role of group and long-term projects. What they are, simply, is a set of general suggestions concerning those aspects of policy that can be informed by the cumulative empirical research and sound judgment. Exhibit 5.3 summarizes these recommendations.

EXHIBIT 5.3 Summary of Homework Policy Guidelines

For districts

Homework is a cost-effective instructional technique. It can have positive effects on achievement and character development and can serve as a vital link between the school and family.

Homework should have different purposes at different grades. For younger students, it should foster positive attitudes, habits, and character traits. For older students, it should facilitate knowledge acquisition in specific topics.

Homework should be required at all grade levels, but a mixture of mandatory and voluntary homework is most beneficial.

The frequency and duration of mandatory assignments should be as follows:
   a. Grades 1 to 3: one to three assignments per week, each lasting no more than 15 minutes
   b. Grades 4 to 6: two to four assignments, each lasting 15 to 45 minutes
   c. Grades 7 to 9: three to five assignments, each lasting 45 to 75 minutes
   d. Grades 10 to 12: four to five assignments, each lasting 75 to 120 minutes

For schools

The frequency and duration of homework assignments should be further specified to reflect local school and community circumstances.

In schools where different subjects are taught by different teachers, teachers should know (a) what days of the week are available to them for assignments and (b) how much daily homework time should be spent on their subject.

Administrators should (a) communicate the district and school homework policies to parents; (b) monitor the implementation of the policy; and (c) coordinate the scheduling of homework among different subjects, if needed.

Teachers should state clearly (a) how the assignment is related to the topic under study; (b) the purpose of the assignment; (c) how the assignment might best be carried out; and (d) what the student needs to do to demonstrate the assignment has been completed.

(continued)

EXHIBIT 5.3 Continued

For teachers

All students in a class will be responsible for the same assignments, with only rare exceptions.

Homework will include mandatory assignments. Failure to turn in mandatory assignments will necessitate remedial activities.

Homework will also include voluntary assignments meant to meet the needs of individual students or groups of students.

All homework assignments will *not* be formally evaluated. They will be used to locate problems in student progress and to individualize instruction.

Topics will appear in assignments before and after they are covered in class, not just on the day they are discussed.

Homework will not be used to teach complex skills. It will generally focus on simple skills and material or on the integration of skills the student already has.

Parents will rarely be asked to play a formal instructional role in homework. Instead, they should be asked to create a home environment that facilitates student self-study.

Annotated Bibliography and References

Annotated Bibliography

Chrispeels, J. H. (1993). *Homework and home learning materials that engage and assist students and their families.* Washington, DC: Office of Educational Research and Improvement.

A guide for helping principals and teachers develop coherent schoolwide homework policies. Includes group activities, handouts, and overheads.

Cooper, H. (1989a). *Homework.* White Plains, NY: Longman.

Cooper, H. (1989b). Synthesis of research on homework. *Educational Leadership, 47*(3), 85-91.

The two publications listed above present the findings of a meta-analysis of homework research. The book describes the methods and findings of the research synthesis in detail. Both publications are the basis for the material covered in this book.

Cooper, H., & Nye, B. (in press). Homework for students with learning disabilities: The implications of research for policy and practice. *Journal of Learning Disabilities.*

A review of research related to homework for students with learning disabilities. Examines how homework policies and practices might differ for students with and without disabilities.

England, D. A., & Flatley, J. K. (1985). *Homework—and why.* Bloomington, IN: Phi Delta Kappa.

Presents lists of homework do's and don'ts for principals, teachers, parents, and students.

Epstein, J. L. (1987a). Parent involvement: What research says to administrators. *Education in Urban Society, 19,* 119-136.

Epstein, J. L. (1987b). What principals should know about parent involvement. *Principal, 66,* 6-9.

Epstein, J. L., & Pinkow, L. (1988). *A model for research on homework based on U.S. and international studies* (Report No. 27). Baltimore: Johns Hopkins University, Center for Research on Elementary and Middle Schools.

In these three publications, Epstein presents both conceptual models for guiding homework and the design and conduct of homework assignments as well as practical advice for administrators.

Foyle, H. C., & Bailey, G. D. (1988). Homework experiments in social studies: Implications for teaching. *Social Education, 52,* 292-298.

Briefly describes the origins and history of homework. Reviews 84 homework experiments conducted in the 20th century and examines their implications.

Keith, T. Z. (1986). *Homework.* West Lafayette, IN: Kappa Delta Pi.

Reviews the homework research literature. Makes recommendations concerning time, grade level, subject matter, quantity, individualization, parent involvement, and feedback.

Lee, J. F., & Pruitt, K. W. (1979). Homework assignments: Classroom games or teaching tools? *Clearinghouse, 53,* 31-35.

Sets out the instructional goals of homework: practice, preparation, extension, and integration.

Leichter, H. J. (Ed.). (1974). *The family as educator.* New York: Teachers College Press.

McDermott, R. P., Goldman, S. V., & Varenne, H. (1984). When school goes home: Some problems in the organization of homework. *Teachers College Record, 85*, 391-409.

Two sources on the more general topic of families as educators, which include revealing ethnographic analyses of how homework fits into the everyday patterns of family life.

Miller, D. L., & Kelley, M. L. (1991). Interventions for improving homework performance: A critical review. *School Psychology Quarterly, 6*, 174-185.

Surveys research on the effects of homework. Emphasizes studies aimed at increasing homework accuracy and completion. Proposes the use of behavior modification techniques.

Turvey, J. S. (1986). Homework—Its importance to student achievement. *NASSP Bulletin, 70*, 27-35.

Brief review of other summaries of homework research and a few individual studies.

References

Anthony, C. P. (1977). *An experimental study of the effects of different amounts of homework upon student achievement in Algebra I, Algebra II and Algebra III.* Unpublished doctoral dissertation, Rutgers University, New Brunswick, NJ.

Austin, J. D. (1976). Do comments on mathematics homework affect student achievement? *School Science and Mathematics, 76*(2), 159-164.

Blackwell, W. B. (1979). *An analysis of the Dial-A-Teacher Assistance Program (Dataline).* Paper presented at the National Urban Education conference, Detroit, MI.

Bradley, R. M. (1967). *An experimental study of individualized versus blanket-type homework assignments in elementary school mathematics.* Unpublished doctoral dissertation, Temple University, Philadelphia, PA.

Connecticut Department of Education. (1984). *Attendance, homework, promotion and retention.* Hartford, CT.

Cooper, H., & Hedges, L. V. (1994). *The handbook of research synthesis*. New York: Russell Sage Foundation.

Cooper, H., & Nye, B. (in press). Homework for students with learning disabilities: The implications of research for policy and practice. *Journal of Learning Disabilities*.

Deci, E. L. & Ryan, R. M. (1985). *Intrinsic motivation and self-determination in human behavior*. New York: Plenum.

England, D. A., & Flatley, J. K. (1985). *Homework—and why*. Bloomington, IN: Phi Delta Kappa.

Epstein, J. L. (1987a). Parent involvement: What research says to administrators. *Education in Urban Society, 19*, 119-136.

Epstein, J. L. (1987b). What principals should know about parent involvement. *Principal, 66*, 6-9.

Fredrick, W. C., & Walberg, H. J. (1980). Learning as a function of time. *Journal of Educational Psychology, 73*, 183-194.

Hinckley, R. H. (Ed.). (1979). *Student home environment, educational achievement and compensatory education*. Santa Monica, CA: Decima Research.

Hudson, J. A. (1965). *A pilot study of the influence of homework in seventh grade mathematics and attitudes toward homework in the Fayetteville public schools*. Unpublished doctoral dissertation, University of Arkansas, Fayetteville, AR.

Keith, T. Z. (1986). *Homework*. West Lafayette, IN: Kappa Delta Pi.

Koch, E. A. (1965). Homework in arithmetic. *Arithmetic Teacher, 12*, 9-13.

Lee, J. F., & Pruitt, K. W. (1979). Homework assignments: Classroom games or teaching tools? *Clearinghouse, 53*, 31-35.

Levenstein, P. (1983). Implications of the transition period for early intervention. In R. M. Golinkoff (Ed.), *The transition of prelinguistic to linguistic communication* (pp. 203-218). Hillsdale, NJ: Lawrence Erlbaum.

Page, E. B. (1958). Teacher comments on student performance: A seventy-four classroom experiment in school motivation. *Journal of Educational Psychology, 49*, 173-181.

Paschal, R. A., Weinstein, T., & Walberg, H. J. (1984). The effects of homework on learning: A quantitative synthesis. *Journal of Educational Research, 78*(2), 97-104.

Pennsylvania Department of Education. (1984). *Homework policies and guidelines*. Harrisburg, PA.

Rosemond, J. (1984). How to help with homework (newspaper article available from John Rosemond, P.O. Box 4124, Gastonia, NC 28053).

Tupesis, J. A. (1972). *Mathematics learning as a consequence of the learner's involvement in interaction problem-solving tasks*. Unpublished doctoral dissertation, University of Wisconsin—Madison.

U.S. Department of Education. (1986). *What works*. Washington, DC.

Walberg, H. J. (1986). Synthesis of research on teaching. In M. C. Wittrock (Ed.), *Handbook of research on teaching* (3rd ed., pp. 214-229). New York: MacMillan.

Wildman, P. R. (1968). Homework pressures. *Peabody Journal of Education, 45*, 202-204.